Choosing a Career in Desktop Publishing

Desktop publishing is an exciting field that involves the design and creation of printed and on-line materials through the use of computer programs.

Choosing a Career in Desktop Publishing

Allison J. Ross

The Rosen Publishing Group, Inc.
New York

Published in 2000 by The Rosen Publishing Group, Inc.
29 East 21st Street, New York, NY 10010

First Edition 2000

Library of Congress Cataloging-in-Publication Data

Ross, Allison J.
Careers in desktop publishing / Allison J. Ross.
1st ed.
p. cm.— (The world of work)
Includes bibliographical references and index.
Summary: Describes the salary, professional requirements, and personal characteristics of those interested in the field of desktop publishing and how the job is changing due to advances in computer software and technology.
ISBN: 978-1-4358-8674-2
1. Desktop publishing—Vocational guidance. [1. Desktop publishing—Vocational guidance. 2. Vocational guidance.] I. Title. II. World of work (New York, N.Y.).
Z244.645.U6 R67 2000
686.2'2544536'023—dc21

00-008570

Manufactured in the United States of America

Contents

Introduction

Computers are everywhere! You have probably seen them in your library or school. Maybe you own one or have a friend who has one. Perhaps you have used one to type an essay for school, to do research on the Internet, to e-mail a friend, or to play video games after school. Whatever the case, you know that computers have many uses, both educational and recreational (for fun). These days many jobs, such as computer technician or software developer, focus on the use of computers.

Maybe you have heard about desktop publishing, another career that involves spending a lot of time on computers. Desktop publishing is an exciting field that allows you to design and create a variety of printed and on-line materials using computer programs. If you are interested in pursuing a career or a job in this field, or you just want more information, it is helpful to know how desktop publishing work used to be done and how it is changing.

These changes have been brought about by advances in computer software and printing technology, and they have affected "prepress work"—work that is done before a written project is printed. Prepress workers used to work with the simple text provided to them by the customer. The prepress worker would take this simple text and use it to format and create a fresh design. By adding new fonts, changing the layout of the text, and inputting graphics, the prepress worker would literally be able to transform the text he or she was given into a more professional and complete work. And because prepress workers developed these new designs, they had control of the design process.

Nowadays, things are different. The customer—in this case, the person who wants to have the material printed—probably has access to a computer. This means that the customer can experiment with the format and design before he or she meets with the prepress worker. Instead of handing the simple text to the prepress worker, the customer can figure out how he or she wants the design, text, and layout to look without the input of the prepress worker. Thus, because the customer is more knowledgeable and experienced, the prepress worker has less input as to what the design and finished product will look like.

The result of all this is that much of the typesetting and page layout work formerly done by prepress workers is now done by customers on their own computers. This change—whereby the design and production of on-line and print publications can be done on computers with graphics capability—is called desktop publishing.

Advances in computer software and printing technology have allowed for much design to be done at an early stage.

Julia's New Interest

Julia wanted to start a nonprofit organization, but she didn't have enough money. Julia and her father drew up a business plan that detailed what she would need to do so that the organization would be a success.

Julia's friend Elijah, who owned a design firm, had a few ideas about how Julia could get started.

"I think it would be good to create some flyers and posters," Elijah said. "That will help you advertise the new company and spread the word. Many people neglect the importance of advertising, so I think this would be a great

start." Because he had all the necessary programs and materials at his firm, Elijah offered to help. Julia and Elijah set up a meeting for the next morning.

But that night, as Julia was fiddling around with her computer, she came up with a few designs herself. As it turns out, she was pleased with what she came up with. In one design, for example, she created a logo using some graphics on her computer. She added a bit of information about the new organization and what she was trying to achieve.

She realized that the most effective posters and flyers would be the ones with as little text as possible. When Julia arrived at the meeting, Elijah had some ideas of his own. He was a little surprised that Julia had done so much work, but he was also quite impressed, especially since their designs were quite similar. They put their best ideas together and came up with some professional and eye-catching designs.

Desktop publishers spend almost all of their time on computers, working to create materials from text files and adding graphics and other design elements.

1

What It Means to Be a Desktop Publisher

In this chapter, we will discuss what is involved in the career of a desktop publisher. You will find out what professional requirements are necessary, what personal characteristics you should have, and what the salary range is.

What Desktop Publishers Do

Desktop publishers spend much of their time on computers, working with files others have created, or with text and graphics that they have composed themselves. They convert and prepare computer files for printing presses and other media, such as the Internet and CD-ROM. Part of this file preparation includes arranging (or typesetting) the text and graphics of the document. Common print publications are reports, brochures, and books. Desktop publishers can also design formats like slide presentations and Web sites. After the file is finished and is ready to be printed, the desktop publisher submits it to a commercial printer, or prints it him- or herself.

It is advantageous for people who work in desktop publishing to learn the many different jobs involved in the work, including editing, production, and design.

Professional Requirements

Certification is not mandatory to be a desktop publisher. In fact, at the present time there is only one certification program that you can take for desktop publishing. The Association of Graphic Communications offers an Electronic Publishing Certificate. The certificate is designed to set industry standards and measure the competency levels of desktop publishing specialists. Although certification is not mandatory, it is wise to take relevant computer classes. In school, English courses and art courses are very important so you can learn communication and design skills.

Most desktop publishers enter this field through the production or editorial side of the industry. It never hurts to learn the many sides of the business, so you might consider trying to learn all that you can. As you work within the industry, you can make connections and build up a clientele.

Personal Requirements

Desktop publishers are detail-oriented, possess problem-solving skills, have a sense of design, and are artistic. Other helpful qualities include patience, flexibility, an understanding of computers, and the ability to type quickly and accurately. If you work as a freelancer, it is important to be able to be motivated and to be able to stick to a schedule. Finally, whether you run your own business or work for a large organization, you must be able to work well with others. Maintaining strong client and coworker relationships is crucial in this field.

Salary and Employment Opportunities

The average wage of desktop publishers ranges from about $11.50 to over $14.50 an hour, and the highest rate is about $40 an hour. The salary range begins at about $18,000 per year, but it can get as high as about $83,000 per year. It is also important to note that the field of desktop publishing is projected to be one of the fastest growing industries. In fact, it is projected to increase about 75 percent by the year 2006. This is good news if you are thinking of going into desktop publishing, as it will make it easier to find a job in this field and will give you more options as you become more experienced.

2

Is Desktop Publishing Right for You?

Now that you have a sense of what is required to be a desktop publisher, let's figure out if you are a good match for a position in this field. To help you figure this out, try to answer the following questions as best you can. By thinking about these questions, you will be able to get a better sense of what the work of a desktop publisher is like and whether this career is right for you.

1. *Do you enjoy working with computers?* Desktop publishers can expect to be on their computer much of the time. If you aren't interested in spending hours on your computer and learning about new technology, this probably isn't the right career for you.

2. *Do you have the patience and desire to learn new computer programs?* Because computer

technology is constantly changing, there will always be new, and often better, software with which to do your work. You need to be willing to take computer classes and learn from your peers. It is also a good idea to talk to those who are in the same field so you can exchange ideas.

3. *Have you been told that you have a good eye for design? Are you artistic?* Although much of computer design can be learned, having artistic talent and a good eye for design can certainly help you do well in this field.

4. *Do you enjoy experimenting with various designs and working on something to make it look its best?* As previously mentioned, a lot of desktop publishing involves learning new programs. But another crucial component is the ability and willingness to play and experiment with new programs. Very often the best work comes from constantly trying out new things—and even discovering them by accident! A good part of the field of desktop publishing involves making a project look visually appealing, so this skill is important.

5. *Are you able to work well by yourself?* Desktop publishing can be solitary work, involving just you and your computer. If you think this might bother you, then you might want to reconsider taking a position in this field.

6. *Does working with clients interest you? Do you think you could listen to a client's suggestions and apply it to your work?* Even though a crucial component in desktop publishing is the ability to work well by yourself, it is also important to be able to listen to your clients. Part of this job involves making and keeping your clients happy.

7. *Can you communicate your ideas well?* You may find that a client is not as experienced at looking at designs as you are and may not understand—or may outright disagree with—what it is that you are trying to convey with your work. Thus, it is important to be able to explain why you did something or why you feel it will work the best, and to articulate your ideas clearly. Since attracting clients and keeping them happy is important, proper communication is vital as well.

Now that you have answered the above questions, you probably have a better sense as to whether or not this field is right for you. Let's talk a bit about the different types of work you can do as a desktop publisher. You could work as a freelancer, which would likely involve working on several different projects at once, for several different clients. Or you might decide to work for an organization or company, where the work is more steady and familiar. Another option is to start your own business as a desktop publisher, which would require you to build up a clientele. Let's

Freelancers are generally self-employed. They take on short- and long-term projects for a variety of different clients, including both individuals and companies.

explore some of these options. Which one would be right for you?

Working as a Freelancer

What does working as a freelancer mean? Being a freelancer generally refers to the fact that you are not affiliated with any company or organization, and that you do short- and long-term projects for different clients. There are many benefits to freelance work. For one thing, because you do not work for any one company in particular, you have a freedom that other people do not have. You can work according to your own schedule and pick and choose the work and projects that you do.

That said, you also have to make a living, so sometimes you might have to accept projects that you are not that excited about. Also, while you can have a more flexible schedule doing freelance work, there may also be lulls where you are not working on anything or have very little to do. Since you may not know when you will land the next big project, these lulls in the working schedule can be quite stressful. Generally, they are filled with trying to get more work and trying to attract more clients.

However, being a freelancer can also be great; you can work on a variety of projects and can meet many new people. One month, you might do a project for a small business that takes two weeks, but at the same time, you also might be working on a six-month project for a large company. This variety can keep your job interesting. Another plus with freelance work is that you can be your own boss, and your work schedule can be quite flexible. You can work from home and can set your own hours. Also, you will have the opportunity to form relationships with a variety of different people at various organizations. All of these different contacts will be useful when networking or trying to find out about new jobs or news in your field.

Is Freelancing for You?

There are many qualities that you need to have to work well as a freelancer. For one thing, are you willing to spend much of your time looking for work and marketing your material? At times, you may have to call everyone you know to look for work, or even call people and companies you don't know. You will also have to schedule meetings with people so you can show them your portfolio. You will be expected to market yourself as someone that the company needs, and to provide reasons as to why you would work well with them. So being able to market yourself and being able to work well with others are very important aspects of freelance work. Also, although you will be working by yourself much of the time, you will need to have good communication skills to better your connections with prospective clients, or even clients you have had for years.

Freelancers must also be quite disciplined. Because you are setting your own schedule much of the time, you will need to be able to make a schedule and stick to it. You must be able to respect your deadlines and to be conscientious about a client's needs and time frames for any given project. If you are contracted to work with an organization on a particular project, you may have to work long hours—and get little sleep—to get the job done. It is important to remember that while you are your own boss in terms of when you work and how you work, you owe it to yourself and your client to do a good job.

Enrique Decides to Be a Freelancer

Enrique has a lot of experience in desktop publishing. Since he graduated from college, he has worked for various organizations in many different positions. This has given him a good sense of the types of materials that people and companies need. For example, when Enrique worked on a political campaign, he learned how to develop various marketing materials and brochures. In Enrique's current job at an advertising agency, he designs and develops print campaigns with other members of the advertising staff.

Saul, one of Enrique's coworkers, asked Enrique if he would be interested in working on a freelance project with him. Because the project was short-term and fairly simple, Enrique decided he would try working on the project after-hours and on weekends.

At first, he found it hard trying to balance two work schedules, but soon found that he enjoyed working on a project that was different from the work he did every day. So it was no surprise when Enrique asked around for more freelance projects to do. It also came as no surprise when he resigned from his job and began to do freelance work full-time.

Working for a Corporation

So what if freelance work isn't right for you? Not to worry—there are other options in the field of desktop publishing. As mentioned earlier, desktop publishers can also work for corporations or organizations. This is a good option for someone who wants to go to an office every day, have a

The steady work flow and exposure to the different types of workers typically found in a corporate environment will help you to gain a lot of experience.

steady and reliable paycheck, and work on projects for one company. Working in a corporate environment can be a great experience because, among other things, you can learn a lot about one industry or field.

Jonathan's Dilemma

Jonathan has worked for a large graphics and design firm for the past three years. In this time, he has earned a reputation for being hardworking and dedicated. He has even won a few design awards for the projects he has worked on. To top it all off, Jonathan also has great relationships with his clients. Not only is he smart and talented, he is also a lot of fun to be around.

"Jonathan is great," says Brad, Jonathan's coworker. "Even when we are working late on a project, or when something goes wrong and we have to start from scratch, Jonathan will always show us that there is a bright side."

Emilia, Jonathan's boss, agrees. "He gets the energy going in this place, and we love him for that," she says. "As an example, a few weeks ago we were all working late on a project; it was after midnight and we still weren't finished. But with Jonathan around, we barely noticed the time. He has showed us all that we can have a little fun while we are working hard, and this has resulted in some of our best work."

But even though Jonathan has a talent for handling people, he was having a hard time dealing with one of his clients, Mr. Rustak. Mr. Rustak owned a chain of stationery stores and was known for being rude and stubborn. While Jonathan tried repeatedly to satisfy Mr. Rustak's requests, it was never good enough. "I felt like no matter what I did, it didn't matter," Jonathan says now. "It was like even if I gave him exactly what he wanted, exactly when he wanted it, it still wouldn't be good enough." Worse still, Mr. Rustak often visited the design firm unannounced. "He would demand to see how his project was going, and then was surprised if he saw that I was working on a project other than his. It was like he thought his project was the only one that mattered!"

Jonathan didn't know what to do. He wanted to say something to Mr. Rustak, but he didn't know how to go about it. While Jonathan was great at dealing with people, he wasn't so good with confrontations. Also, he was worried that he would offend his client and knew he could potentially lose his business. So Jonathan asked his coworkers for advice. They suggested that he try to sit down and talk to Mr. Rustak—letting him know that while his business was important, they had other clients who were important, too. So Jonathan did just that—and to his surprise, Mr. Rustak apologized! "I couldn't believe it," says Jonathan. "He said he was sorry and that he didn't realize he was being so demanding. He even admitted that he thought we were doing a great job."

As we saw in Jonathan's case, having coworkers around is a great benefit of working in a company or organization. Not only can you develop great relationships with them, but you can also give each other support and help. Let's look at Jonathan's experience again. Without his coworkers' input, he probably would have continued to put up with Mr. Rustak's rude behavior. But Jonathan's coworkers helped him realize that the best way to deal with the situation was to talk about it, and the situation had a great resolution. While Jonathan didn't have much experience with confrontations, his coworkers did, and they helped him figure out what to do. Coworkers can also help you with your projects, offering advice and opinions, or even helping you get the work done. And don't forget, coworkers can be terrific resources. You can learn from each other and teach each other new things.

You would do well working for a company or organization if you work well with others and enjoy coming in to work at the same place every day. You might work for a firm that specializes in desktop publishing and graphics, or you might work for a company that has its own design department. For example, many large accounting firms have their own design groups. These groups work on in-house materials, reports, newsletters, and presentations, to name a few. The "clients" in such a company are the employees who work for the firm—not people from other organizations that have hired you.

As with all aspects of desktop publishing, it is important to be detail-oriented and to like working on new projects and designs. It is also important to stay on top of the latest computer programs. Sometimes companies will offer free computer classes to their employees, which is a great benefit for someone in this field.

Starting Your Own Business

Those who start their own businesses often have a lot in common. They tend to be energetic and

You will probably like the environment of a company or organization if you work well with others and enjoy coming to the same place every day.

hardworking, and have a great desire to succeed. Having good ideas is also an important characteristic, as is the desire to learn everything you can about the field you are about to enter. If you are thinking about starting your own business, you should make sure you are well prepared. It would be difficult to start a desktop publishing business when you don't have much experience or knowledge about the field; thus, it is probably best to make sure you are well versed in desktop publishing before making this leap. Years of experience are invaluable when you are starting a business.

A True Learning Experience

Wilhelmina was in her second year of college when her best friend, Phoebe, had her nineteenth birthday. Wilhelmina, whose nickname is Winnie, made Phoebe a birthday card on her computer. She designed the card using the graphics that came with her new computer program, and played around with the fonts until she found the perfect one. "When I was finished making the card, I thought it looked great," says Winnie. "I couldn't wait for Phoebe to see it."

Later that night, Winnie and some of Phoebe's friends threw her a surprise party. They all had some birthday cake while Phoebe opened her presents. "A bunch of people saw the card I made," says Winnie, "and they were all really impressed. By the end of the evening, I was convinced that this was what I was meant to do for a living. Before I knew it, I was sure I had enough skills and know-how to run a greeting card company."

Winnie dropped two of her college courses so she could start a part-time business. She tried to learn as much as she could but found it difficult to do schoolwork at the same time. After three months, she gave it up. "I still want to run a business, but I realized I don't know enough yet," says Winnie. "I plan to do it later in life, after I have had a few jobs and know all aspects of the field." Also, Winnie says now, she will wait to start a business until she has developed some contacts and a network of people she can learn from.

Having years of practical, hands-on desktop publishing experience is invaluable when starting your own business.

As Winnie discovered, having lots of experience really helps when it comes to starting your own business. Generally it is smart to have years of practical experience in desktop publishing—working in various situations or for various companies so you can learn all aspects of the field. For example, if you have experience only with designing annual reports, you probably aren't ready to start your own business. You need to have design experience in several areas and experience with the financial side of business as well. You can't run a company unless you know how the bookkeeping works, how expensive it can be, and how to budget properly.

Even if you have years of experience, you should keep talking to people so you can get and keep contacts in the business. Since technology is constantly changing, keeping in close touch with other desktop publishers can help you stay on top of what's current. You should also be sure to speak with those who have started their own businesses. They can give you tips on how to start your new venture and can let you know about the types of challenges you might encounter.

Have You Got What It Takes?

Starting your own business requires lots of drive and determination, and it can be quite unpredictable. While you will need to work very hard to get the business established, you may not see the financial rewards for some time. Thus, patience and confidence in yourself and your business are crucial for success. Starting your own business also requires creativity, as you will have to come up with ideas to set your business apart from all the others. Because you will spend a lot of time explaining to others how your business can help them, marketing skills are also quite necessary. As with freelance work, being able to stick to the schedule you make for yourself is also very important.

3

Projects for Corporations and Organizations

Perhaps you have experimented with some design or graphics programs. Some of these programs are very easy to use and are made especially for beginners. For example, the program might show you how to create a design step-by-step and might give you certain choices as to what graphics and fonts you would like to use. You may have already learned that you can use a regular black-and-white printer to print out your finished work, or you can use a color printer.

So what are some other things you might design in your work as a desktop publisher? In the next few chapters, we are going to discuss work you can do for a company or organization, print and on-line publications, and creative materials.

Let's start with work you can do for a corporation or an organization. You might work on a project that takes many months to complete and that is distributed to the company's clients or shareholders. Or you could work on a project that lasts only a couple of weeks, such as designing advertisements to be placed in the local paper. Whatever the project, doing work for a corporation or organization can be exciting and a great learning experience.

Some of the more common materials you can produce for a company include annual reports and proposals, business forms, corporate identity systems, collateral and marketing materials, and presentation graphics.

Annual Reports and Proposals

Companies need desktop publishers to design annual reports and proposals. An annual report is a document that companies use for promotional reasons and to report the finances of the company (public organizations are required by law to provide financial information each year). Annual reports provide a summary of operations for the past year and the financial standing of the organization. They also include other information about the company, such as its future plans and profiles of key staff members. Charitable and nonprofit organizations and schools publish these reports as well. As a general rule, these reports are distributed to those with an interest in the company, such as partners, investors, customers, and/or employees.

Let's get a little more specific. Pretend that Sam's Toys, a popular toy store, has asked you to design their annual report. What type of information would the report include? For starters, the

Desktop publishers must design reports for corporate clients that are clear and visually appealing, presenting complicated statistics in a way that is easy to read.

report would mention how many toys were sold that year and how much profit the company made on those toys. There would likely be some photos of the toys in the report as well. You would probably be asked to create some charts and graphs to supplement the report's findings. The report would discuss these statistics for the previous year and perhaps even some of the company's plans for the future. Companies generally include a letter from the chief executive officer (CEO) of the company, or an article on a top executive who played a large part in the company's success for that year. Also, there is always a letter from the auditor certifying the financial results that are in the report.

The job of the desktop publisher is not to provide the specific statistics about the company's business; the company will supply this information. However, it is the job of the desktop publisher to design the report so that it is clear and visually appealing. It is also the responsibility of the desktop publisher to ensure that the overall appearance of the report matches the client's needs. One of the challenges of designing an annual report is to turn statistics, numbers, and complicated information into something that looks visually appealing and is easy to read.

Some companies, especially large ones, produce their annual reports "in-house." This means that they have their own design group that works within the company to produce their reports and materials. If you are a freelancer, you might have luck finding work in this area if you approach smaller companies and nonprofit organizations that have limited budgets. Keep in mind that annual reports may take a considerable amount of time to produce, and you may have to deal with several individuals or departments within a company that will be providing input to you. This means you will most likely have to do many revisions of your work. However, there are definite benefits to this type of work, such as the fact that a company can be a good source of repeat business. Once you develop relationships with individuals within the firm, it will become that much easier to be hired for additional projects and work.

Another type of report that companies often produce for prospective clients or investors is called a proposal. Proposals outline the company's ideas and explain the services that the company offers. Companies may also produce reports (for internal or external use) that outline their plans and research. Depending on the scope of the report, the company may want a formally designed layout with charts, illustrations, or photos.

Business Forms

You can also produce business forms for a company or organization. Business forms are those used internally by a company, and some forms are also seen by customers and other people. Business forms include documents such as invoices, order forms, routing slips, statements, and customer satisfaction surveys.

Designing a business form may not sound too challenging. After all, it generally involves a fair bit of text and probably no graphics or photos. But designing forms can be quite challenging. First, you have to make sure that you design a form that is easy to read and fill out. Also, if you make these forms more attractive and unique than the generic forms that are often used, you may have a better chance of convincing a company that they need you to design new forms for them. Getting companies to realize that they need new—and improved—business forms can be tricky. A good approach might be to talk to your current customers about designing new forms for them and to provide them with a few reasons as to how these new forms will help improve their business.

Corporate Identity Systems

A corporate identity system is a term that generally refers to logos, letterhead, and business cards. Because these items are so common and are used so frequently, the design of corporate identity systems is something that needs a lot of thought.

Company logos are very important to companies. For one thing, logos help people quickly identify a company or organization. Let's use the McDonald's symbol as an example. You can probably recognize their symbol—the giant "M," or "golden arches," as they are commonly called—without having to see any other marking or identification. In other words, you don't have to read the name of the restaurant to recognize what

Desktop publishers also design more creative materials for corporate clients, such as logos, letterhead, business cards, and brochures.

the restaurant is. The golden arches help customers identify the restaurant before they see it and set McDonald's apart from other restaurants. Logos are used in almost all printed materials a company produces. Along with color and other basic design elements, a logo can reinforce an organization's identity and the public's awareness of that company. Try to think of other company logos that you know. You will probably be surprised at how many you can think of.

Letterhead and business cards are the basic items that most businesses use and are often the first thing that small business owners will contact a desktop publisher to create. For a small business on a tight budget, the letterhead might also be used for printing invoices, flyers, or even for simple brochures. If you are working with a new or very small business, you might want to show them various designs that allow them to use their basic letterhead for a large variety of other documents.

Collateral and Marketing Materials

Collateral materials include a wide range of documents that companies use to promote themselves. They are generally designed to provide ongoing public relations for a company. Some examples of collateral materials are brochures, flyers, and posters.

There are many types of brochures that you might be asked to design. You might work on a brochure that introduces an entire company and its products or services, or one that focuses on a specific product. Also, companies may have a variety of brochures aimed at different types of customers—prospects, new customers, and repeat customers, for example.

Flyers and posters are other examples of collateral materials. They are often used to announce special events or sales. Other promotional materials can include notepads, calendars, bookmarks, magnets, and T-shirts—basically anything that provides long-term exposure for a company. These items generally have the company's name, logo, and contact information imprinted on them. Specialty businesses often create some of these promotional items, but some businesses may hire a designer to create a special design. If you worked on such a project, you would likely work with the specialty printer directly.

Desktop publishers also work on marketing materials, including advertising materials and direct-mail packages. Direct mail refers to anything from simple letters to postcards to complete packages with letters, brochures, order forms, and other promotional items.

Presentation Graphics

Companies often need help with presentation graphics—visuals that are used to supplement a meeting, speech, or presentation. Years ago, presentations were often just speeches, or speeches with overhead projections or slides. Because technology has advanced, presentations now often include many visuals that accompany

Small companies often hire freelance designers to create multimedia presentations.

the speech. A presentation graphic might be a simple PowerPoint (a computer program that is used to create slide shows, etc.) presentation or a complicated multimedia presentation. A multimedia presentation might include videos or music, for example. You also might have to create some technical illustrations, such as graphs and pie charts. Because many people know how to create PowerPoint presentations, it is more difficult for freelancers to find work in this area. Also, many larger companies handle their presentation needs in-house. If you are interested in this area, you might try to find some work by assisting small companies or individuals who need to make presentations.

4

Print and On-line Publications

In addition to projects for corporations and organizations, you might be interested in working on a print or on-line publication. Print publications include things like newsletters, magazines, books, and menus. On-line publications include things like e-zines (magazines on the Internet) or Web sites. In this chapter, we will discuss periodicals, publications, self-publishing, catalogs and menus, and Web and electronic publishing.

The *Williams High Reporter*

Janet loved to fiddle with her computer. But what started as a casual hobby turned into something that she grew to be quite skilled at. In her junior year of high school, Janet had an idea: She wanted to create a school newspaper. Her school, Williams High, was rather small and had never had a school newspaper before.

Janet was convinced that with a little help she would be able to head up the project. She read a few books on the subject and took a computer course after school as well. The course taught her how to use QuarkXPress, a computer program that is often used for creating documents. By the end of the course, Janet knew how to lay out a few pages of a document complete with columns, page numbers, and photos! She showed her final computer project to Miss Elan, her English teacher, who fully supported Janet's idea of a school newspaper. Miss Elan took it to the school board the following Tuesday, and the idea was met with much enthusiasm by all members of the board. Better still, the board petitioned the budget team for some funding for the project, and the budget was approved. With the money, Janet and Miss Elan were able to purchase the latest computer programs to help them design the best newspaper possible.

Janet rounded up some of her interested class members to report on school events and write stories. Three months later, the first issue of the Williams High Reporter *was published!*

As mentioned in the introduction (and as we just saw with Janet), anyone who has access to a computer and who has some relevant computer skills can design and create materials using a computer. As with anything else, the more knowledge, materials, and skills you have, the higher the quality of the items you can produce. In Janet's case, she was able to create a document and print it out in much the same way that a newspaper does, with columns and photos. Janet took a course to learn how to use a specific program so she could complete what she set out to do.

Periodicals

Periodicals are publications that generally come out on a regularly recurring schedule, whether it's once a year, once a month, or even daily. Can you think of some types of periodicals? If you thought of newsletters, newspapers, and magazines, you guessed right. Because these kinds of materials are published on a regular schedule, this type of work can provide the opportunity for repeat business. Keep in mind, though, that this work can be very time-consuming.

Depending on the type of periodical you are working on, you might produce a newsletter that is a simple, one-page document produced from your desktop printer. Or you might work on an elaborate four-color publication, like something you would find on a newsstand. Magazines and newspapers are less commonly produced by freelance desktop publishers. However, as a freelancer, you may be able to obtain contract work for special sections of larger publications. Smaller publications or those with daily publishing schedules may be more

Desktop publishers create periodicals—newsletters, magazines, newspapers, and zines—on a regular schedule for both corporate and private clients.

Books and manuals are designed and typeset by desktop publishing professionals.

willing to hire freelancers for some of their design and production work.

Publications

The term "publication" refers primarily to books and other nonperiodical works, such as booklets, workbooks, and manuals. Whether you are working at a company or as a freelancer, typesetting for a long document such as a book generally requires professional-level tools. Adobe FrameMaker and QuarkXPress are considered the leaders in this field for these types of publications. Because freelance desktop publishers sometimes wear many hats, you may also have to do some technical writing. Normally, however, these jobs are done by professional writers.

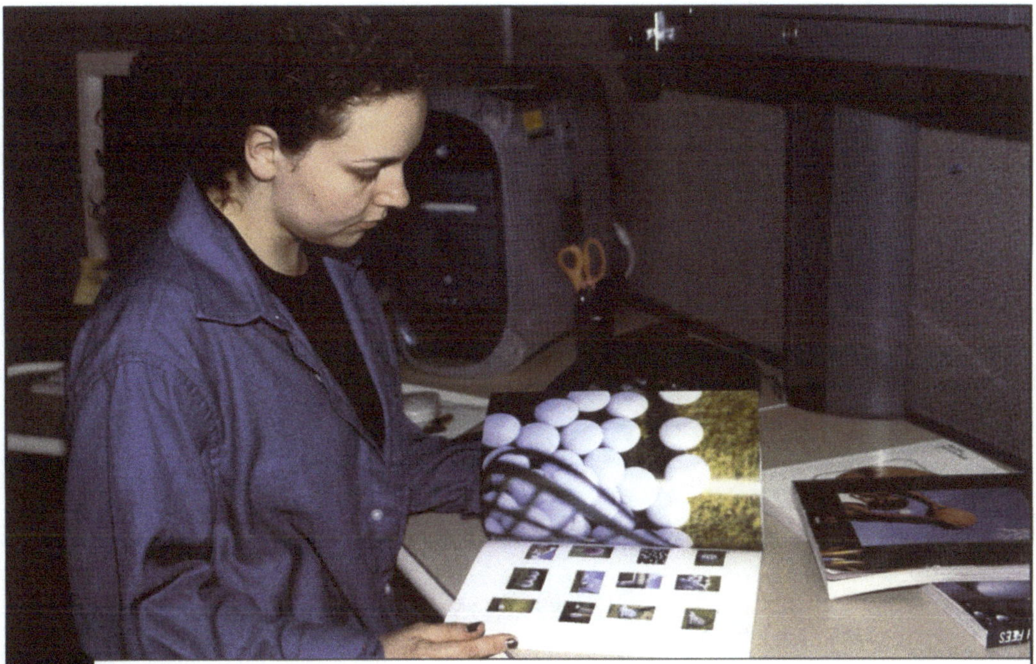

Self-publishing is generally done on a small scale, often for promotional purposes.

While major publishers often handle all book design and layout, freelancers may be able to find some work by providing these services to self-publishers or small independent book publishers.

Self-Publishing

Self-publishing is the for-profit publication of books, newsletters, booklets, and other publications. The main difference between self-publishing and desktop publishing is that you are self-publishing items that you sell, such as a book you wrote, or a subscription-based newsletter. Some self-publishing may be done to supplement another business. For example, a self-published customer newsletter can be aimed at increasing business or generating sales of other products or services. Some

Opportunities in Internet and electronic publishing, including jobs in Web site design and on-line editing, are growing all the time.

self-publishers even require the services of desktop publishers to do design and production work.

Catalogs and Menus

Any company that produces a number of products or parts for sale is a potential customer for your catalog design skills. Generally, catalogs consist of illustrations or photos with descriptions of the products depicted. Catalogs can be large or small, ranging from small booklets to bound books of hundreds of pages of items. Also, catalogs present an opportunity for repeat business because product lines and prices often change frequently.

You can also do design work for menus. Menus range from simple price lists to elaborate booklets with photos and illustrations. As with catalogs, restaurant offerings and prices change often, which can result in repeat business for you.

Web and Electronic Publishing

Some people think that Web and electronic publishing may one day replace print publishing. Until that happens—if it does—Web publishing will simply remain a major facet of desktop publishing. Web publishing can involve designing Web pages or entire sites, providing original content, or placing existing print documents on-line.

Electronic publishing includes Web as well as other nonprint publishing, such as e-mail newsletters, CD-ROM publications, and eBooks. While some Web and electronic publishers come from a print design or desktop publishing background, many enter the field without any prior training in desktop publishing, graphic design, or traditional publishing. If you are interested in Web and electronic publishing, it would be a good idea to take some courses in Web design. This area of study is relatively new, and there is plenty of need for experienced workers in this area.

5

Creative Materials

Working on annual reports for a company or designing a Web site can be very creative work. But there is another side of desktop publishing where creativity is important in two ways: both for the actual design that you are doing and for the format you are working with. For example, let's say you are designing some party decorations. You would need your actual design to be creative, and you would need to be creative with the materials you choose for the design. Some creative projects might be small, such as designing an invitation to an event. But while such projects might not have big budgets, they are very important to the businesses and people that rely on them. In this chapter, we will discuss crafts and creative printing, signage, packaging, and publication art.

Crafts and Creative Printing

Computer-generated crafts can be income-producing businesses. For example, you could sell your creations on-line or at craft shows. Many

These young entrepreneurs might see an increase in sales with the advantage of signage designed by a desktop publishing professional!

creative printing projects can also be used as promotional items and giveaways by small businesses. Some of these items might include calendars, greeting cards, invitations, envelopes, scrapbooks, and party decorations. Although professional page layout and graphics programs can be used, there are a huge number of specialty programs aimed specifically at this market.

Signage

Think about all the places where signs are used. A retailer needs a sign to put on his or her store. A hotel needs signs to mark the elevators and the front desk. Cities and states need road signs. Even individuals need signs for their garage sales or for a lemonade stand. You can probably think of many more.

For some types of signage you'll need to become familiar with local or state regulations regarding size, acceptable symbols, and even the type of fonts you can use. Although your designs may not be printed on paper, even metal, plastic, and neon signs can be designed on your computer. Adhesive decals, bumper stickers, and novelty license plates are also a part of this category.

Packaging

Packaging is an area that covers everything from labels to bags to boxes of all shapes and sizes. While you might produce labels from your desktop printer, most packaging production is done by specialty printers. However, you can design the artwork with page layout and graphics software.

If a company produces a product, it generally needs packaging of some type. Boxes for software, food and wine labels, product tags, and shopping bags are just some examples of packaging that can be designed by a desktop publisher.

Publication Art

Publication art includes magazine cover or book jacket designs, custom illustrations and photography for books or periodicals, and technical illustrations. Sometimes the desktop publisher may be called upon to provide the artwork in connection with a publishing project. They may contract with others to provide the artwork, or they may specialize in a certain type of artwork—

providing their services to book or magazine publishers directly or through another designer. This area is not strictly graphics. It also includes typography and page layout for covers and inserts, among other things.

While many larger publishers handle the artwork in-house, one market to explore is the creation of jacket designs and artwork for smaller self-publishers or CD inserts for smaller independent bands and music publishers.

6

How to Get Started

No matter what career decisions you make, it is important to remember that the decisions you make don't have to be permanent. You may think that you want a career in desktop publishing, for example, but then realize it's not for you. Or you might start off thinking you have an interest in design work for publications and periodicals, but then decide that the Internet is where you would like to focus your work. That's okay, and it's completely normal. It is important to be happy and to do something that you enjoy; if you are dreading doing your work every day, perhaps you should think about doing something else.

That said, desktop publishing is an incredibly exciting field, and one that is right for many kinds of people. Read the papers and take out books on the subjects in which you are interested. Read everything you can so that you can make informed decisions. Even if you aren't looking for a new job, it is smart to read the classifieds from time to time. This will give you a sense of the types of jobs that are out there. You

It is a good idea to regularly read newspaper and on-line classifieds, even if you aren't looking for a new job, to stay informed about the types of jobs available.

also might want to try looking for a job on-line; there are many Web sites that list job opportunities and want ads.

The growth of technology has made the Internet an exciting forum to do design work—a space where creativity is key, and work is plentiful. The Internet is also a great way to advertise your business and highlight your work. With a click of the mouse, everyone can see what type of work you do and how well you do it. This is a terrific opportunity to attract more customers and to help your business grow.

Finally, if you are enrolled in computer classes, talk to your instructor about job possibilities. You can also talk to others enrolled in the class; someone may have some good ideas that you have not thought of. It is important to keep your eyes and ears open for new opportunities. Above all else, be patient! Jobs in this field are plentiful. You just have to find the perfect one for you.

Glossary

CD-ROM Compact disc that functions as a read-only memory.

certification Taking a course or program that satisfies certain requirements. When a person is certified, this means that he or she has completed a course of study or may officially practice a specific profession.

charitable organization Organization that gives financial or other aid to the needy.

chief executive officer (CEO) The highest ranking executive in a company or organization.

desktop publishing The design and production of on-line and print publications done on computers with graphics capability.

freelancer One who sells his or her services to employers without a long-term commitment.

Internet Matrix of networks that connects different kinds of computers around the world.

investor One who commits money in order to gain profit or interest.

invoice Bill that contains an itemized list of goods shipped or services rendered, with an account of all costs.

layout Making a detailed plan of printed matter and how it is going to look (such as for a newspaper or book).

portfolio Materials representative of one's work that are often carried in a portable case that holds drawings, papers, and photographs.

prepress work Work that is done before material is printed.

proposal Written explanation of an idea or of research.

shareholder Holder, or owner, of a company's shares of stock.

Where to Go for Help

In the United States

Art Directors Club of New York
106 West 29th Street
New York, NY 10001
(212) 643-1440
Web site: http://www.adcny.org

Association of American Publishers
71 Fifth Avenue
New York, NY 10003-3004
(212) 255-0200
Web site: http://www.publishers.org

Association for Suppliers of Printing, Publishing,
and Converting Technologies
1899 Preston White Drive
Reston, VA 20191-4367
(703) 264-7200
Web site: http://www.npes.org

Graphic Arts Technical Foundation
200 Deer Run Road
Sewickley, PA 15143-2600
(800) 910-GATF
Web site: http://www.gatf.org

Graphics Communications Association
100 Dangerfield Road
Alexandria, VA 22314-2888
(703) 519-8160
Web site: http://www.gca.org

Independent Computer Consultants Association
11131 South Towne Square, Suite F
St. Louis, MO 63123
(800) 774-4222
Web site: http://www.icca.org

Society for Technical Communication
901 North Stuart Street, Suite 904
Arlington, VA 22203-1822
(703) 522-4114
Web site: http://www.stc-va.org

In Canada

Association of Web Professionals
6299 Airport Road, Suite 706
Mississauga, ON L4V IN3
(905) 673-0003
(888) INFO-AWP
Web site: http://www.a-w-p.org

Canada Council for the Arts
350 Albert Street
P.O. Box 1047
Ottawa, ON K1P 5V8
(800) 263-5588 or (613) 566-4414
Web site: http://www.canadacouncil.ca

Canadian Advanced Technology Alliance (CATA)
388 Albert Street
Ottawa, ON K1R 5B2
(613) 236-6550
e-mail: Inquiry@cata.ca
Web site: http://www.cata.ca

Interactive Multimedia Arts and Technologies Association
789 Yonge Street
Toronto, ON M4W 2G8
(416) 926-9301
e-mail: imat@imat.ca
Web site: http://www.imat.ca

For Further Reading

Bonime, Andrew and Ken C. Pohlman. *Writing for New Media: The Essential Guide to Writing for Interactive Media, CD-ROMs, and the Web.* New York: John Wiley & Sons, 1998.

Brownstone, David M. *Complete Self-Publishing Handbook.* New York: Penguin, 1999.

Crumlish, Christian and Malcolm Humes. *Web Publishing with Netscape for Busy People.* Berkeley, CA: McGraw-Hill, 1996.

Devall, Sandra. *Desktop Publishing Style Guide.* Albany, NY: Delmar Publishers, 1998.

Fanson, Barbara A. *Start and Run a Profitable Desktop Publishing Business.* Bellingham, WA: Self-Counsel Press, 1997.

Kalmar, Veronica. *Start Your Own Zine.* New York: Hyperion, 1997.

Kursmark, Louise. *How to Start a Home-Based Desktop Publishing Business.* Guilford, CT: Globe Pequot Press, 1999.

Parker, Roger C. and Berry, Patrick. *Looking Good in Print* (Fourth Ed.). Scottsdale, AZ: The Coriolis Group, 1998.

Seidman, David. *Exploring Careers in Journalism*. New York: Rosen Publishing Group, 2000.

Snell, Ned. *Easy Web Publishing with HTML*. Indianapolis, IN: Macmillan, 1998.

Toore, Marcelle L. *Graphic Design on the Desktop*. New York: John Wiley & Sons, 1998.

Index

Credits

About the Author

Allison J. Ross lives in New York City, where she works in communications for a professional services firm.

Photo Credits

Cover photo © Superstock; pp. 2, 21 © R. W. Jones/Corbis; p. 8 © VCG/FPG; pp. 10, 25 © Superstock; p. 12 © Ronnen Eshel/Corbis; pp. 17, 43, 45, 46, 53 by Maura Burochow; p. 27 © David C./Corbis; p. 32 © Rob Goldman/Corbis; p. 36 © Stephen Simpson/FPG; pp, 44. 39 © Telegraph Colour Library/FPG; p. 49 © Annie Griffiths Belt/Corbis.

Design

Geri Giordano

Layout

Cynthia Wiliamson

www.ingramcontent.com/pod-product-compliance
Lightning Source LLC
LaVergne TN
LVHW070625061126
851857LV00002B/14
* 9 7 8 1 4 3 5 8 8 6 7 4 2 *